THE GEM-IN-I:

A Journey Through Self's Center

Vol.1

By: El-Yoshuah Malahki

Library of Congress

Cataloging-in-Publication Data is available upon request.

ISBN: 979-8-9861707-2-5

Written, Edited, and Published by: El-Yoshuah Malahki
Edited by: Priestess Nuna Ma'Khai
Front Cover Art: AI generated image using ChatGPT (powered by DALL-E)
under the creative guidance of El-Yoshuah Malahki

Social Media Pages:

Instagram, Tiktok & YouTube: @elyoshuahtheprophet
Facebook: El-Yoshuah Malahki

CopyrightDepot.com number 00094972-1

ABOUT THE AUTHOR

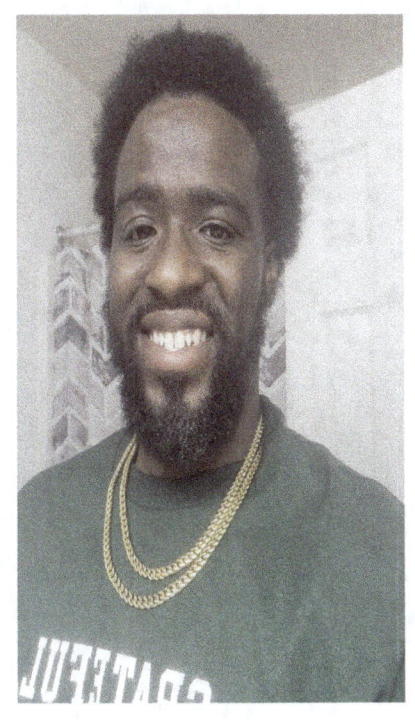

El-Yoshuah Malahki was born and raised on the west side of Baltimore. He is a father, author, poet, and motivational speaker. He self-published his first book titled, *EYE AM By: Joshua Seldon* on 27 August 2022 (currently available on Amazon and Barnes & Noble). He was inspired to expand his creativity by writing poetry and sharing with his peers. The focus of *"THE GEM-IN-I: A Journey Through Self's Center Vol.1"* is to storytell through rhythm and rhyme poetry. He takes us on a journey through his childhood and adult life in a unique form of poetic expression. He reveals his childhood experiences, trauma, self-love tips, and a series of events that took place throughout his life in a bold, imaginative and inspiring way. Yoshuah was inspired to share the roots of his pain with the collective in hopes that it would inspire them to reflect and create spaces for healing. He relentlessly commits to sharing wisdom and encouragement to help others free themselves of the pain and suffering that keeps them from progressing and thriving in life.

Words from the poet:

I hope my poetry encourages the collective to share their stories in a way that promotes healing and growth. One of my greatest wishes is for the world to experience healing, which requires that we free ourselves of past experiences of pain, suffering and trauma. Sharing my gifts and talents helped me to heal tremendously. I hope that by immersing yourself into this poetry book that you no longer feel the need to hide and lurk in the shadows. There is a community of star seeds that accepts you for who you are. I love all of yall and I hope that we can commit ourselves to grow and unite to raise awareness on the importance of healing individually and as a cosmic community. May we all live life to the fullest daily in abundance. You have always been looking for you. You just didn't know it... Until now. Embrace every aspect of your being. Continue to be the change you want to see in the world. Ase'

Self's Journey

The journey through self awaits...

Pressure

When the Stars Aligned

Spring cracked the sky.
Summer ushered its way in.
It was a little after noon
It might've been a sunny day.

Darkness filled the space
but light was moments away.
I've outgrown momma's womb
as my arrival soon to manifest.

Behold—another sun was born,
weighing just over seven pounds.
I bet my mother smiled
While rain dripped from her clouds

The nurse foretold a prophecy,
but time had to run its course.
The clock struck its final dial.
Behold, the last was born.

My name holds value.
No middle came between the two.
Sacred texts were written that day,
as the stars aligned in trine
connecting Mercury to the Tenth House.

Communication, prophecy, truth.
All of it destined
to tell the story
After all, it's a blissing

Because life has a funny way
of showing you
who you already were
at birth.

Quiet

Whispering wind
calms the reign of darkness
Silence fills the air

Summers Left Behind

As I sat and watched my siblings leave,
left behind poor young me.
Like a quarterback throwing on 2nd and goal,
while the running back silently rides the bench.

My action figures filled a friendly void;
we laughed, we giggled, we played
until the day fell asleep.
But once the toys were put away,
loneliness crept in
like fading light beneath bold skies.

The next day, bitter oatmeal filled my pain.
I pushed it aside but still
the bowl had to be put away.
"TO THE WALL", I cried.
and there went the oats, sliding in pain.
Shame on me,
for letting my anger fall away.

My toys returned, my friends again.
Here we go... with this again.
At least I smiled for a moment or two,
before the skies turned dark blue.

Hole in the Wall

We were play-wrestling during summer's blaze.
The bed stood tall.
The sheets were gray.
You tried to dominate me
NO, No, no...
Not today.

A dropkick from heaven soared,
to knock the hell out of you.
Back up off me!
I still had work to do.
Pausing to tame my breath.

Drums rumbled in our chest
as you grabbed my foot in defiance.
I wiggled my finger.
KaBOOM!
A dropkick rearranged your face.

You still couldn't overpower me
not until we pushed each other off balance.
Then came the strength of a thousand bears.
To the wall you flew,
wearing a stunned stare.

Ooo, I'm telling Dad
annoyingly repeated
a mix of blackmail and fear
echoing steps in my head.

No longer guilt-bound
until weakness crashed back in
Let the hole in the wall
tell its side of the sin.

Why Would You?

Why would you?
Too embarrassed to speak a word,
suffering in my silence
like burned paper turned ash.

I highly favored you
Even when Dad stayed on you
A hard head made a soft behind.
Still, I often paid for your crimes.

I trusted you to buy me shoes.
I even left you clues.
Eastbay magazine marathons in my mind,
as if asking for something was a crime.

Out came the opening act
as the audience flooded the sofa.
You said we looked alike
Then humiliation introduced itself.

In front of everyone
you pulled my pants to the ground,
shivering for my body.
My underwear screamed for me.
Why would you decompose my innocence?

Laughter erupted in the room.
So did my tears
raining quietly on the floor.
The embarrassment became the closing act.
How did that make you feel?

That's a scar that stayed sealed
until I undress the wound.

Transformed my pain to steel
while liquifying my feelings.
It stayed buried with my youth
until it rose again
while taking a toll
on my mental strolls.

B-More Careful

A city that never sleeps
with cameras on every street
Take a trip to Mondawmin Mall,
ferry rides at the harbor,
Lexington Market food quarters.

Long walks to school,
with no bus in sight.
Either Dad dropped us off
or our legs got a jump start
on P.E. for life.

Damn near late
every other day.
It was a hike or two
felt like walking a 5K.
Ain't no joke
in the heart of the city.

Visits to the park
near the airport's breeze.
Value City for the Avirex jeans.
Edited hip-hop CDs,
PS1 with Tekken Tag dreams.
GameStop runs
on after-school steam.

Those were the days
except for breathing in
that factory musk.
Constantly clearing nostrils
of smog-thick dust.
City air built lungs
that couldn't be crushed.

Mom loved downtown shopping trips
dentist appointments
and doctor visits.
That retainer went to war
with my back teeth
until my hand wiggled them
free from the barricade.
That retainer
didn't stand a chance against me.

Reminiscing
rats rattled trash cans.
Cats got chased
down alleyway paths.
Milk crates?
Best rims we ever had.

Never on Sundays
with checker paper baskets.
Mortal Kombat arcade battles
Can I get some tokens please?
I'm about to beat the game
while lunch settled
warm in my belly.

Across the street
the laundromat hums.
Sub shop next door
got the hood smelling numb.
Philly cheesesteaks paraded the block.

Pigeons laid resting
in the field near the lot
until my brother
splashed water
and they shot off like rockets.

My fears?
They shook me.
Thought a pigeon
might peck me
while poop dropped
on bold heads in the mist.

I laughed the scare away
with a stomach full of bliss.

Uncharmed City

Slumbers sweep the street
Through the police siren's shouts
Unsettled debts rage

Shy

I remember when my presence was silent
no one cared I was there.
Like air taking up space
Lonely set in at times.

Until the stares came
those weird, wondering faces.
Nerves kicked me out my mind,
and fear whispered in my ears.
Oh, how wonderful they sounded

Curses rolled off my tongue.
No turning back now.
The damage had already taken course
and the fight invitations followed,
like sealed letters from karma's courier.

If only Shy had sat me down,
I wonder what life could've been.
But pain was a passage
and out came the lion from within.

Suspension walked me home.
Three fights in one day.
Whew. That was a blast!
And just like that—
we packed our lives into boxes
Virginia was calling.
A shift shaped by my shadow's cast.

The NEW Kid

Suffering from homesick
New grounds to cover
Fresh was my name for awhile
At least until the summer

I sat alone
until friends traveled into my life
Felt amazing
until the smells wore off
Then I became the jokes
from others insecurities

She would never date me
Even if money was involved
Words never talked a word
My silence was loud
I was hated for my looks
Teased for my sense of style
Until another newbie came around
There presence was greeted

Guess that was a tough crowd
Boo!, erupted in my head
Volcanic thoughts spewed out my mouth
When will school be let out?

Spring Aries in
Gemini fooled around
Not looking forward to Virgo
I guess my rising sign will tell

It's Just Another Day

My solar return rotated in
happy to see another cycle.
Light filled the sky
as the sun smiled my way.

School sailed smoothly,
like a crisp pair of new shoes.
I couldn't wait to get home
to see what gifts would come through.

A smile raced across my face,
matching the brightness of the sun.
Hey, he just winked at me!
What a beautiful sight to see.

Racing home with joy and excitement,
I danced through the door.
A cake stole the table's shine
Could this day hold more?

Along came my eldest brother
the masculine version of our mother.
I told him what day it was.
He paused and uttered
It's just another day.

My heart shattered into puzzle pieces.
Time put them back together.
Those words echo in my ears
Subconscious documented my fears

We couldn't have been raised
by the same mother.
You were the star of the show
on your special day.

Yet you stole my light away
brought sis a gift,
and took bro to the movies.
But when it came to me?

I was the guilt
that made you diarrhea
from your mouth like shit.
I bet soap tasted better.

Bitterness sat heavy in my spirit
You sowed a seed
that grew into a tree.
It wasn't for you
it blossomed in me.
Which left you
overshadowed by jealousy.

Years later a text
Shattered your ego
It left you puzzled
Truth sat you down
Reflection stepped forward
If only respect was non-negotiable.
Would you have listened?

Summer's Heat

Sweat met the ground's blaze.
Rainbows shimmered in heat waves
as if the rain
had gone on vacation,
while heat
suffocated the planet.

Deserted throats cried for water.
Salt spilled from our pores.
Washed towels and t-shirts
still smelled of
early rising shower dates.

AC couldn't bear the heat.
Bodies packed into curtained rooms
game graphics on screen,
while Arizona Arnold Palmers
quenched thirsts
as water went on strike.

Gloss gleamed
on Cadillacs, Ford Explorers,
and Monte Carlos.
Hardee's had the best car shows
showroom clean
on gravel lots.
The city boomed
of subwoofers and tunes .

Football at the park
was a breeze
interception, then fumble
to our knees.
Tackles hit like ice coolers,
while the old heads

blazed grills
of hamburger and hotdog dreams.

The wind steamed
of Mars air
but we didn't care
to complain
unless stillness
froze the day like glass.

Portable hoops ruled the streets.
21 and pickup
Long range jump shots
Pretty girls playing hopscotch
with sundresses and crop tops

If only summer
stayed a little longer.
If only school
didn't call us back.
Maybe Fall
would appreciate that

But the world
just kept spinning,
folding time
inside itself.

It was fun
while it lasted.
Now
school shopping,
the endless rotation,
until someone flips out
the Infinity Loop.

I'll never take back
what summer gave.

Each year
housed new adventures
while the world
steadily evolved.

Cheers to the '90s babies.
Look how far
growth has come.

90's Babies

Summer was golden
when life became our playground.
Shaved ice froze our chests,
blue dye tattooed our tongues
sugar crashed through our veins.

How could we forget
when outside meant everything
Football spirals carried air.
Hoop dreams echoed
on roundabouts,
with bricks holding rims
'cause water jugs weren't enough.

Cookout smells simmered the atmosphere,
seasonings activated our senses.
Ketchup, mustard, cheese
a cookout dream from yesterday,
a taste stamped on our generation.

Parks were flooded with joy.
Everyone vibed.
Even water danced with us
ice was its sidekick,
as bodies rolled dice in summer's heat.

Then came the old heads
card tables, checkerboard cloth.
Slapping cards like gang signs,
yelling, *Boston!*
Game over.
A beautiful time to be alive.

Busch Gardens trips,
lazy rivers at Water Country,
Kings Dominion coasters

and Six Flags visions
spinning in my mental dreams .

Remember the group walks?
Corner stores and Save-a-Lot hauls
donut sticks, barbecue fritos,
tall Arizona's—peach or watermelon,
Domino's pizza as the night's king,
video games, anime,
nostalgia stitched into memory.

The 90s was a blast
Fun is what we had.
Grew up fast,
but the memories marched on,
passed down to the next rotation.

Now we relive it
this time with our seeds beside us,
healthier plates,
sweeter lessons,
but still letting them explore.

Not too strict
They deserve their own joy.
But 90s babies...
Do you remember that?

School Daze

You ever wonder
why school consumed us
as if some bounty
was paid to keep us asleep.
School resembled prisons
A mental daze with slave conditions

If only kids
were taught to use
more of their mental magic.
Instead of wreaking havoc

Sitting for hours,
Dazed by mind shackles
except rubber bands,
paper hornets,
and who could hit the back of the neck
before the teacher turned around.

Learning from old textbooks
that never told *our* history.
Science was the only time
you could smell the flowers.

Day in.
Day out.
Wasting every hour.

Wash.
Rinse.
Repeat.
A wash cycle for the mind.
Where our brains
were wrung dry.

Unless you enjoyed the lesson,
test day had you stressing.

Writing up research papers
about unsung heroes
who might've never existed.
Funny what lies
books can sell.
Until you write your own.

Filthy bathrooms smelled
like mildew and markers.
Graffiti from silly kids
tattooed the stalls.
Janitors probably chuckled
at least when the principal wasn't looking.

Lunch ladies were dope.
Until one took her job too seriously.
Then turned around
and gave away free snacks.
If only the lunch reflected on
The essence of home cook meals

I cruised through homework
while history played boring beats.
So daylight could meet me after school
breaking tackles with grass filled cleats.

Walks to Save-A-Lot
donut sticks and Seagram's ginger ale.
Glass-bottle sodas hit better,
no debate.

Then came the crack of dawn,
especially during daylight savings.
Who invented that nonsense?

Dragging my body
to the bus stop,
but the cutie made it worth the wait.

Crowded bus.
Holding your seat
like a sacred ground.
Damn near falling out
before we hit the school lot.
Friends posted up
fiending for free breakfast.

Should've eaten at home that day.
pancake sausage on a stick
frozen,
drenched in grease.
my stomach cartwheeled
before first period.

Twelfth grade
felt like a stretch
Classes got so boring
I let storing take my test.
Drool betrayed me.
Laughter erupted
from the second floor.

Band class next door,
class clown in full form.
Still kept the grades tight.
Report cards hit different
until 10th grade science
almost welcomed me back.

Last day of school?
You couldn't tell me nothin'.

I showed up
freshest of the year.

True Blue Jordan Retro 3s.
Superman graphic tee.
Camo shorts
matched the elephant print.
Evo Slide Sprint phone
in my back pocket.

Saturday afternoon approached.
The defining moment.
Diploma in hand.
School,
finally over.

Until
adult school
stepped in.
Because when one chapter closes
a new one
always begins.

Formation

My First Love

I set my intention
bold and clear.
I wanted a woman I could spoil.
P.O.F., get over here.
I've got a fish to catch.

I threw out my line,
reeled it back a little.
The bite of a
lifetime appeared.
She was bittersweet
and a tall glass of wine.

We harpooned to Larry's.
The food? To live for.
My cheekbones did pushups
they were mashed in the gravy.
The picture came out blurry,
but those moments were divine.

Pink dolphins
swam the waves of my chest.
Ken Griffey
struck out my feet.
Khakis laid smooth on my legs.
Tattoos paraded my skin.
Glasses shaped my vision.
And my smile?
Gifted.

Makeup slayed her skin.
Dimples married her cheeks.
A Cheetah gift wrapped her neck.
Trees glamoured her legs.
Shall I detail the rest?

Dinner faded.
Fountains called our names.
We wandered the city center
benches hugged us close.
Kisses of fire and air
Sailed through the skies
as if Mars was conjunct with Mercury.

I loved it here.
Can we marry under the moon's light?
Let the universe carry our wishes
as stars journey across the sky.

Trooper carried us away.
Streetlights kept us awake.
We forgot the ice cream
Remember?
It was getting late.

I'll ice cream scoop you later
You texted me paragraphs.
I teleported my heart to you.
My eyes?
They double dared you.

The rain started laughing.
Rio planked the parking space.
Fog swallowed the interior.
Wood imprinted Levi's.
Juice buttered thighs.
Moans met the atmosphere.
We couldn't have felt
more alive.

During the seventh cycle
Life took your essence away.

Memories became movies.
Isn't that an epiphany?
The world... was what you meant to me.

Do the stars align with a trine?
you were playing music
through your eyes.
The universe
made you my symphony.

May the ancestral realm
treat you well.
Your sweet scent
I still smell.

I know death
meant well.
You were only
escaping hell.
Was that you
who rang my bell?

Peer Pressure

Absolut consumed my liver.
Never again
Then came the magical plants
as I stumbled out of my body.

Microwaved mashed potatoes
became a five star cuisine
while scalding my chest to death.
The mark buried itself under thick skin.
I'll let hurt tell the rest.

The second test.
vibe lit up my day
until pizza rolls spun my stomach
like a rinse cycle.
Hot Pockets joined the ride.

I felt three of me
walking at the same time.
Wait, it's my turn to give directions.
Then my mind sat me down and said:
You've had enough for today.

Third time's a charm.
You won't get me today.
Until peer pressure pulled up again
waiting to get his lick back.
You ain't finished yet, my friend?

Out came a surprise in 2020.
All my friends arrived
including Peach Paul.
He entertained company.

Drinking went on vacation.
But peer pressure?
He made a house call.

Hello old friend.
What are we getting into today?
Is it the high of highs?
The slurs that keep slurring?
The jungle juice
jumping into jams?"
My body followed the crowd.

 Peer pressure whispered:
My friend, I'll never let you down.
I'll always lurk in your shadows.
Just don't leave me hanging too long.
You know I hate being stranded.

He never gave up
trying to impress me.
I slowed down
but only for occasions.

Peer pressure and I
became good friends.
Except this time
I make the exceptions.

Soles Journey

Detroit Piston Black 6s.
Food Lion checks earned that flick.
Hall of Fame turned into 1s again
Citi Trends flooded my closet.

eBay followed my wallet home,
for a date with Cherry 13s.
Even the 12s couldn't resist me
my foot had its own scene.

Mall visits to Finish Line,
Foot Locker refereed my shoe game.
Recording highlight tapes,
sneakers hinged my closet door in place.

I think we had an issue.
Tissue blew the shoebox nose.
The Flu Games were contagious.
No full-court pressure tho.

eBay once again came knocking
used gems in rotation.
Penny Half-Cent my purchases.
collection so glorious,
Kool-Aid couldn't match these variations.

Cranberries with suede molds.
Eggs planted firmly on my toes.
Silver surfed its way home.
Royal Blue won the game show.

Lime Green's postgame interview
came with anthracite commissions.
This story checked out long ago
laying flat on shoebox pensions.

Doernbecher 2s in highlight reels.
Aqua 8s came strapped with wheels.
My feet?
They practiced polygamy.
Had multiple wives
in sneakerville.

Moonlight

I manifest new
Chambers of truth and life goals
Dreams reveal rewards

Special K

June welcomed
a pre-summer seedling
swimming the tides
of a wombed portal.

There go the twins
in one small body.
Light enough
to fit in my palm.

Two pounds, seven ounces.
Traffic kept me from delivery.
If only I had traveled faster.
A phone call
delivered my seedling.

Tubes breathed life into his lungs.
Steroids fed strength through lines.
Light as a feather
born a warrior.

Jaundice lamps
coppered his pigment.
He craved Mama's
liquid melatonin.
He sprouted longer each day
as if that lamp
imitated the sun.

I remember changing
dark-poop diapers.
Almost got some on me
laughs erupted
through the nursery.

He was just
clearing toxins out.
Eventually.
brown movements came.
We stayed at
the Ronald McDonald house
yet no chickens clucked,
no cheese doubled.
Home beds
felt better.

Frequent nursery visits
became the norm.
Traffic couldn't keep us away.
Special K needed our love
more than the nurses could provide.

Three moons past
summer's rest
a car seat away
from the welcome party.
He lay pressed to
turquoise patterns,
gems twined
father and son.

The reunion:
family as one.
Trials came soon after,
but that day
told a different story.

We birthed
the next greatest artist.
Oh, how time
has raised its ages.
Eight

the cycle of renewal.
The path of least resistance.

If only his Mom
could see his progression.
Instead,
her personality
lives within his genes.

Generational Trauma

The waters of futures past
runneth deep in our cells,
memories imprinted
from those who came before,
and passed down
until someone dares
to break the chain.

Dad nearly met death by an axe,
fighting cold nights for shelter,
the forest his only refuge
'til Auntie played mama
because his father never gave a damn.

That pain didn't end, it spread.
His rage spilled into his seeds,
eruptions at unexpected moments
fists flying, rooms clearing,
the wrath of wounded gods
unleashed through blood.

Mama suffered in silence,
murmuring to herself
visions no one wanted to hear.
She was born with foresight,
her intuition vivid and sharp,
delivering messages
that chilled me to my core.

Pneumonia kissed her twice.
Once after the fire,
once post-dentist chair.
She carried sickness like shadow,
but wore strength like sunlight.
I never saw her fold.

Now, I've come
to rewrite this story.
To speak the unspoken.
To break the curse.

I am the axis
where the chain finally snaps.
Allowing our pain to depart
without a stain.
I release it all
for them, for me, for what's to come.

Bold Expressions

The sense of joy
dwells deep within your being
igniting the eternal flame
of passion, purpose,
and bold dreaming.

You express it in divine form,
sending radio-wave signals
through the open hearts of listeners,
who rise from the crowd
to stand in awe
of the greatness reflected in you.

You are the gifted
wrapped in presence,
adorned with ribbons of gold,
sprinkled with a mother's love.
How radiant is the light you hold?

You gather the weary,
transforming broken thoughts
into blueprints of purpose
guided by third eye's vision,
whispering truths
from the well of intuition.

The divine ones listened.
They feel your presence
glow within the room
like high beams cutting through
a pitch-black country back road,
showing the traveler the path ahead.

You float within the mind's vast wonder,
weaving visions with patience and care
crafting a world worthy

of Gods and Goddesses,
Remembering their inner knowledge.

Be the voice that shatters chains
those locked tight
around imprisoned minds.
Where trauma once whispered,
now the truth speaks.
The pain?
It finally swam away.

The inner temple of your spirit
calls for its time in the spotlight
projecting your sacred visions
onto life's silver screen.

You speak to crowds
of awakened kings and queens,
wide-eyed and wide-open,
soaking in your frequency
as it reverberates
through stadium walls.

Balance returns to the world
as ancient temples rebuild,
this time with a modern flame.
The Universe writes a new equation,
with infinite answers floating in.

We are who we've been waiting for.
The aboriginal beings
—the organic light,
returning to claim
this sacred Earth once more.

Release

As pain walks itself out
wholeness enters like still breath
to realign the mind's roots

Chiron

Healed in sacred flames,
the seeker leads with purpose
channelled divine will

Self Reflecting

Thoughts flash like recent memories,
as if yesterday pressed
play on my past.
Emotions flooded my organs
like a cannon blast with no casing,
just impact.

Mercury retrograde whispered chaos
my ribs simmered,
my gut boiled,
like a mudslide after a tsunami,
waves crashing through
the fragile coasts of my mind.

Sour rage lined my throat,
like biting a key lime
with no tequila in sight.
Salt slipped the rim,
searching for refuge
with nowhere to rest.

Clouds pierced the silence,
distorted commentary
from shadow voices,
thoughts tossed in mental trash cans.
Mercury sure had a field day with me.

Storms went on vacation
with the moon's shadow
Baggage claim overflowed
I overpacked for this flight,
but it wasn't meant for me.
It was for the parts I buried
my subconscious rode
a first class flight
to the depths of my soul.

I called my power back.
Recollecting my strength.
Wounds breathing.
Owned every scar,
tattooed my pain
with tears that carved new skin.

The hurt felt treacherous
But the comeback?
Felt divine.

When I finally looked outside,
I dove headfirst into the flames
the sun planted
garden beds in my heart.
Seedlings rose
from the depths of my soul
and with them, reasons to grow.

Cuddling pain became heavy,
So I spread my wings
and soared.
With my aura
lighting the way.

Long. Lived. A Dream

Excited to be back in school
the fool's journey has just begun.
waiting on my chance to shine,
hoping actions weighed a ton.

No résumé, just high school days,
a few small tryouts in my past,
but faith stood up with courage bold,
and made that long shot cast.

I reached out to the coach
with hope clutched in my chest.
No promises, no guarantees
just gave that dream my best.

My thoughts outran my body,
already dressed in win and glory.
I spoke belief into my bones
was already telling my story.

Leave it all out there. Don't hold back.
Let your grind do all the talking.
Spring arrived in summer's skin,
and the heat kept watchers gawking.

Tryouts came. The drills began.
Pain showed up in streaks.
But healing followed close behind,
with strength sewn in my cleats.

The stint was short, the snaps were few,
but every bruise held gold.
I played the game I dreamt about
let that truth be told.

I learned what pads can't always show:
Leadership,
Teamwork,
Brotherhood,

and one deep gem that still burns bright
I fulfilled a dream.
I made it real.
I gave it life.

Then came the shift
my spirit caught a new route.
Football faded
as a higher path spoke out.
No more first downs,
my soul called a timeout.
The game was just the spark
but passion lit the whole house.

→ *Purpose entered the chat*

Reflection

I remember when I first noticed you
low dark caesar,
crisp edge-up,
round face, chin held high.
Flexing muscles
with Kool-Aid smiles,
bushy brows,
patterned shirts in a photo lens.

Innocence glowed in the city
just a young kid
In a rough city.
But I always
kept a giant smile.

School dazed
my memories brain
Fistfights puffed my chest with pride
standing tall nearly
broke my stride.
after three strikes,
suspension called me home.
Computer class
fueled raging bulls.

Teen years?
Gravy.
Honors glazed report cards like pastries.
Math bent the angles of my mind.
I raced through homework mysteries
so daylight could meet me after school
breaking tackles in grass-filled cleats.

Graduation?
A patriot's cap, a tailored gown.

Another chapter
bowed itself down.
Adulthood knocked
and I stood there still,
meeting its gaze
with iron will.

My reflection smiled,
a silent nod.
He'd seen the boy
grow into God.
A caterpillar shed its shell
the old skin gone
Life's mystery
still spun my thoughts.
What's next?
But answers fought.

Gather your mind,
let waves arise.
Let life lift you
to open skies.
Spin magic's thread,
and forge your gold.
Stay the course.
Let the truth unfold.

Family calls
and trauma bleeds.
But healing plants
its buried seeds.
Your light still shines
your gifts are proof.
Don't miss life's call.
Become your truth.

Let curses lift
like feathers fall.
There's balance
in the weight of all.

When the mirror
calls you through.
Remember,
I am just a view
of the higher you
that always knew.

Checkpoints

The road less traveled
revealed my inner strength
The paint faded the path
a map slithered from my hands
Where am I going?

Though I walk through
the valley of strays
where the unknown lays
Sleeping on elevated floors
Paste across the shadow walls

The black dot at the end
Spins uncontrolled with
shining assortment of lights
beaming far behind the path
What is my assignment?

Travel the path
with the unknown presence
of mind wondering
What's to happen next?
But don't whisper a clue
because the journey spoke for itself

As I kept traveling
The revelations of your heart
Erupted from the sun rays
with a cliff hangers thrill

Shivering for adventure
There lies a steep hill
Climbing up the mountain side
with a hint of heart pulses

Racing through my veins
waving through my hands
As if patients took a day off
Not long after the checkpoint

Waving a green flag
Chanting my success to the universe
With more journeying to go
How much longer do I have?
A lifetime, perhaps
— and then some

The Great Awakening

It was the worst cycle of my life
at least, that's what my nerves said.
To bear the tragedy and pain
whispering through my temples.

My hands folded my glasses like clothes
and threw them into the underworld.
Rivers flooded from my eyes
as the dam of my hurt collapsed

He should've stayed indoors,
instead of stalking the bus
as if school was approaching,
he just had to venture out.

Out came the monsters
that threatened to steal my son.
Until higher forces intervened
before the emergence of the drought

I never thought Thursday
would present me my last hug,
with kisses of mocha cookie crumble.
The sweet aroma soothed my heart.

The call I wasn't looking for
showed up after a subtle rest.
There goes that drum
beating out my chest.
I gathered myself
to fly up north.

Only to be met by a broken collar bone,
and tears erupting from my son.
I couldn't leave his side.
The inner hero showed up that day.

Sirens left me puzzled to pieces,
trying to calm the storm
before thunder escaped the clouds.
Behold, the silent room of terror.
Why am I sitting here alone?

Doctors swarmed the room.
Scrubs filled my headspace.
My glasses escaped my hands
the floor swallowed the frames whole.

My eyes showered rainwater.
Voices rumbled the ceiling.
Headaches drowned my brain
as my thoughts checked out the emergency room.

Is this a dream?
Has reality tricked me again?
Did I commit a terrible sin?
Wait, when did this all begin?

It was after my 21st solar return.
I remember how the flowers sang.
I reached through the concrete
to grab her hand
but she met me with a handshake.

I remember it like yesterday.
memories couldn't calm my pain.
It ran a 5k through my stomach
The hurt carried my breath away.

rained swept roads that day,
While the ethers carried her away,
pouring tea cups of pain
into the waiting room of silence.

I had to learn how to look again.
My eyes held onto a heavy burden.
Pardon my French
I hated the fucking feeling.

I ran until my mind gave in
tempted by the thoughts
of being left alone with my fears.
Libra showed up later that year,
Tipping the scales of life.
I was losing a war
I wasn't prepared to fight.

October's harvest carried me.
A social media post
ignited the hermit within
Leading me to rewrite
the pages of my heart.

The universe heard
my cries for months.
I guess she got tired of the voicemails
or maybe I mistook imagination
for intuition.

A new chapter was written
blank pages laid before me
for my magic to flow in
through the power
of my pen.

Hidden

Mentals Health

Pressure-washed walnut shells.
Frequent day trips to hollow wells.
Bridges collapse
thoughts with no borders dwell.
Breaths turn seconds
into timeless spells.
A windless race
a mind without rails.

Crash course to the frontal lobe,
confronting waves where shadows strobe.
The battle of the century
moments fade into memory.
Wills testify
to bury trauma's mental health,
until higher forces
intervened.

The inner warrior showed its face,
Wounded Leos found its grace.
Twelfth-house slices,
a pie of dreams,
a journey through the mind's extremes.

We hit a wall!
A running back's fumble.
Play-action stalled,
then calls would crumble.
Quarterback draws
Iso'd at mid-field.
Wait a second.
How did we get here?

Mercury's retrograde played charades,
Geminis shrugged while Virgos bathed.

We're hitting critical mass
Captain, where are we headed?

Sail the great seas
for treasures unseen,
from subconscious isles
and in-between.
Mate, be keen.
Mountains slip when they gleam.
Caves breathe of
intuition's dream.

Which port do we enter?
Who claims the call?
Shadow, is that you
lurking through it all?
Don't drift too far
Chiron lanterned Leos' core.
The heart-space glows
like never before.

Careful, lad.
Saturn has returned.
Boundaries inked.
Lessons learned.
We must return
the tides pull strongly.
Piscean waves
sing boundary songs.

Tie the boat,
but not too tight.
The moon's still young.
We sail by night.

Wait! Captain—look!
The Gem-in-i map!

We hold the route.
Prepare to unwrap.
Northern node,
Sagittarius' flame.
Why there?

That's where purpose came.
The trail of Aries
leads us home
a path to self
etched into stone.

Tides will spark.
Let fire be known.
Ride intuition
let fear be thrown.
Oh, Captain
we've just birthed a superstition.
Once we dock,
chakra mediates.
The deeper you breathe,
the more truth awakes.

My astro-body
drifted back to bed.
My journal grinned,
and softly said:

Today, self-love stopped by to stay.
He whispered life
in a sacred way.
And that, my friend,
was food enough for the day.

Anger

War erupts through your body
depleting energy.
while internal waters
bubble and boil.
The lining of your stomach
Burns the waste
You refuse to release.

If Aries battled Mars,
The outcome would be devastating
collapsing timelines into
volcanic spills of
stone and flame

You skip stones across ponds,
Disrupting water's rhythm.
When scorpion's sting
meets sub-zero ice,
another battle brews.

Elements wage war,
forgetting they exist
to bring balance and harmony
How could you miss that?

Pounding and swinging fists,
threatening to cave in chest,
leaving bodies breathless
on the floor
The spirits of clubs
thirst for more.

Give rage a rest
before you

dwindle to ash,
muscling through
every phase
like a fist-fighting shadow
inside a dancing flame

What about the mirror you shattered?
Did it deserve your rage?
It can't piece itself together.
It only reflects
fractals of this reality.

That was a cheap shot.
Now your pockets
watch you bleed.
Pouring out cash
to replace your downfall.

Channel that sacred flame
Into something divine.
Let poetic rhymes
be your release.
Typing until your fingertips
leave skin on keys.
But at least your building
instead of breaking.

Remember:
anger is just a mask.
Take it off.
Let it rest.
Maybe today you failed the test.
Try again when
you simmer down.

Water deserves your softness

even when it rains
from your inner fountains
dripping through the threads
of your layered skin

Let the heat dry it up.
Balance is synchronistic
when you choose to bend
the energy,
instead of penetrating it with
force and resistance

Open up.
Peel back those
layers slowly.
If you pull too fast
you'll miss
The one that needed
your deepest attention.

Be patient with yourself.
Step away
From what doesn't serve
Let your inner hermit
Bring clarity
within the chaos.
Be the change
You once tried to burn.

12 Feet Deep

Subconscious portals
through depths of introspection
where shadows crept voids

Weathering The Storm

Heavy rain.
Stormy nights.
Winter storms.
Snowy flights.
Wishes awaken
beneath summer's light.

Stars spill softly through the night,
Dwelling beneath its silver light.
It's lonely here.
The silence calls from deep within
Will her soul with mine collide?

Screaming voices
won't settle much
Cursing me out
while I simmer my lunch.
Lighting candles
with sacred intentions
wasn't enough.
Felt like I'd lost
my magician's touch.

Through the storms
of past situations,
the fog cleared
only to let
more floods in.

Can I keep warm
on the rooftop of my doubts?
Maybe revisit
my grave of weakness?

Wills reveal
all the pains
that humbled me.

The water scalded
my heart's shattered pieces.
Puzzle parts drifting
into creeks of regret.

The keys
left floating away
in rivers
of unfortunate events.
Will these storms
ever subside?
Can the lessons
just step forward,
make its final remarks?
This story's getting too heavy.
Fussing fears
has had enough.

Mom told me
to pray through the storm.
But my mind drifted
far from her warmth

The depth of pain
gripped me in its arms
dragging me
toward the slopes of hell,
entrenched
in the dark night
of my soul.

Will I see
the light of this
again?

The Mission

Reserved for the strong,
even in moments of weakness
blistered feet still march
on buried bones,
breaking ground beneath cracked secrets.

When midnight's train comes whistling,
my laptop glows like moonlight's flame,
pulling me toward passion's tug
through rough patches
with one eye half-awake.

Fatigue takes the blame
as energy leaks from tired hands,
spilling thoughts across the canvas
but *Don't give up*
Continue watering those flowers.

Temptation taps at the gate.
Heart pounding
like a thousand hooves
the road clears,
and courage grabs the wheel.

Traveling through cliffside dreams,
eclipsing doubt in mountain curves.
My inner engine roars to life,
building form from molten rocks.

Skin rips like fragile bark,
muscles rise in sculpted truth,
'til cantaloupe veins burst
through the biceps of will
strength carved in natures fruit.

The lion enters,
wise, roaring through life's reps,
walking tall through grass fields
that grew from grit
and sweat-soaked steps.

The breakthrough is near.
No quitting.
Mouths wait to feast
on the crops of persistence.
Just a few more miles
before divinity lands.

The finish line glows gold.
Ancestors rise, clapping rhythm
into my bloodstream.
My team huddles
the play call of the century.

And then—BOOM!
The game-winning drive ignites.
Tunnel vision sharpens the sky.
I ISO the ball,
no defender in sight.
Only the stadium lights.

I cross that line,
the crowd erupts
and victory echoes.
But was that enough?

Falling Backwards

Y'all were there for me
more then
Even when my heart was laid to rest,
with songs beating through my chest.

You gave me a safe space
to be myself.
Even when I lost touch
while traffic raced through my thoughts.

When I started my healing journey,
spirit sat me down
Until my sun started shining again
brighter, softer.
I hope you innerstand my stance.
I was working on myself

Please don't take it personally.
I was learning how to put myself first.
Living rent free in my thoughts
Wrestling with self worth.
At times I felt overworked.

Let me release my stress.
Drink a sparkling water
burp out the pain
as if that could erase the hurt.

Y'all didn't do anything wrong.
It was me. I'll take the fall
if it leads me
up my elevator to self.
Isn't that what I asked for
after all?

Mending broken relationships
swallowed my mind.
I sat too much.
Didn't go out for light at times.
Just me, wrestling with the void.
Let me explain more,
if that's fine

I'd been doing for others
more than I did for myself.
After I left my last 9 to 5,
attention divorced my feelings,
I masked my pain
with a sneaker addiction.
But slowly
I became more self-sufficient.
Discovering my intuition.

Then came imagination,
wild and untamed.
Sensitivities arose.
Emotions numbed my body.
My absence became a safe haven

FaceTime calls stretched long.
Reconnection felt like
catching up in a marathon
I was severely losing.
My mind wandered through the fog
until clumsy me had a great fall.

Self-reflection paid me a visit.
I sat.
We talked.
And after the conversation,
I couldn't believe
I'd done all that.

That's what happens
when you fall back.
Welcome home.
Self whispered that.

Apologies started to pour
while anxiety babysits my thoughts.
That's what your love opened.
I was today years old
when I saw it clearly.

My shadow took me on a date
and set the record straight.
Answers danced through dreams.
My journal planted seeds.
At times
I fell to my knees.

I wrestled with depression.
But I never signed the contract.
I consulted with my feelings
and they agreed to fall back.

Everything I've written here?
All facts.
I spent some time
sitting with that.

The Foods Journey

What's on the menu?
Is it crispy-edge pancakes
with pan-fried scrapple
or whole cake bread
with salmon cakes
Maybe save-a-lot chicken patties
with stiff and flimsy cheese.
Can you hand me the ketchup and mayo?
Double-decker me, please.

What about deep-fried gizzards?
With hot sauce and ketchup,
and a side of wedges
so I can hear my jaw crumble.
Now I want pan-seared salmon.
Better yet, I'll oven-roast it.
With flaky crisp skin
I learned that from my mother.

Time for a change-up.
Let's incorporate some salad
drizzled with balsamic vinaigrette.
Now that's more like it.
No, no, no
My body needs more nutrition.
Craving hummus wraps
on naan with falafel,
slices of avocado,
and a drizzle of garlic aioli.

Bring out the ninja blender.
Cut up some watermelon
with a slither of key lime.
What a refresher for the soul.
The aroma hugged my nose.

Let's be bold.
Try a water fast
Followed by a dry fast.
How long do you think that'll last?

 My body found relief
when I dialed back eating meat.
Now I'm sipping coconut water
with a berry smoothie
sweetened with dates.
I'll treat myself to an acai bowl today.

But what about music?
You consume that too.
The vibration affects your mood.
Death and destruction
 don't sound too cool.

Solfeggios ringing in my ears.
The winds of the beat
combing through my beard.
While my mind tickles
with the greatest of ideas
That's soul nutrition.

Don't forget your surroundings.
People can be toxic.
Some ain't really vibing with you.
Don't be fooled by the energy vampires
climbing through dreams,
hovering over your chest,
sucking your life force dry.
Who's filling up your

Be intentional
with your thoughts.
Right now is the perfect start.

Don't overwhelm yourself.
Take your time.
Cruise the journey.
This path was built just for you.

Breathe
or your face glows blue.
Bathe in the sun
to strengthen your hue.
Are you listening to the cues?
This is music to your ears
like rhythm and blues.
Which side will you choose?

Let your heart guide you.
Watch transformation unfold.
Give yourself gentle touches.
Pause to drink nature's essence.
Fall in love with where you're at.

Every chance make changes
that create lasting effects.
After all, this is your life
Are you facing the facts?

Surprise!

Willing to conquer my quest,
I overcame fears
and strengthened my breath
lifting heaviness off my chest.
The work became my mission.
I weeded through premonitions,
tuned into my senses,
and fulfilled long-held wishes.

Reflection mirrored my flaws
the shadows stained my shirt.
Raspy voices whispered
camera shy, I hid my worth.

Still, I gave myself grace.
Picked up life's pace.
Faced terrors head-on
Coach called me in the third.
I dropped seven points
and shook the Earth.

Walk through many faces of healing.
Wrestled thoughts like dice on ceilings.
Left a paper trail in journals
recordings of inner dealings.

Magic worked through winter's cold.
Rivers spoke where streams flowed.
Tow-truck progress reports
delivered by heart's receptionist.

Food for thought:
watermelon-lime juices.
Creative meals
where alchemy moves through wooden spoons
transformation in the kitchen's womb.

The journey felt complete
but my mind escaped the tomb.
Grief became my quiet friend,
lifting burdens
off my chest again.

Push-ups grew bolder.
Legs painted the carpet.
Gratitude breathed through every pose
dancing stagnant energies around
until they rose.

Early rising messages.
Group therapy confessions.
Spilling meaning to the sun
on black streets
with scrambled legs
toe outlined shoes
winning silent races.

Confidence became
my living testimony.
Fire erupted
from volcanic membranes.
Fasting led the way
the soul's journey
toward everlasting flame.

Are we there yet?
No...
It's only
the beginning's beginning.

Break-Fast

At one point,
pancakes and sausage with sage
had me deep in a daze
glazed with maple syrup,
orange juice in a chilled glass haze.

Don't forget the buttery slope
that sat atop a mountain of flapjacks.
Crispy edges kissed by flame
each forkful
sent you drifting in a dream.

That was the first meal
but not the first deal.
See, we break our fast
with fruit or water
not bread and high fructose corn syrup.
That slow silent killer
got you cursed
by your ancestors' food laps.

Setting the tone,
puppeting your mood
left you dazed,
sleepy,
slumped.

You just woke up
and already
you're heavy with clouds
and pork scraps.
What was the purpose in that?

Break fast.
Break the fast
with an 8oz glass of water

followed by fruits like
watermelon,
strawberries
Cucumber lime water
to revive your temple.

Purging out toxins.
Erasing the lies.
Clean out your colon
like the Browns
superbowl dreams.

Worms left speechless.
Folded like bad bets.
Put the fork down
next to the napkin
of poor decisions.
Let water
enhance your vision.
Let fruit
dance with intuition.
Make it a daily mission
to water your internal garden
waking your bladder,
so your colon can semi-truck
waste down the expressway
without stressing the toilet.
Give your body a break
from years of detriment.
Let it rest
from the cold after cold,
from the burden
of always catching up.

Your body needs a blissing —
a reset,

a restructuring
of sacred cells.

So you can rise
From a descending hell
and eat your way
into heaven.

Balance of Scales

Tipping scales of time
remembered visions
spun gold into passions

Grape Vine

A seed that grows
even when the lights are off,
racing through the soil's
hidden halls
beneath the surface,
it knew the climb was worth it all.

The light peeks through
or has the seedling grown
A toddler now,
above the ground
curious, reaching,
feeling home.

Rooted deeply
in Earth's embrace,
it waves at the sun
with a vine-skinned grace.
Light kisses limbs
that stretch and sway,
drinking in each golden ray.

There go the arms,
reaching skyward wide,
as heaven's rain
slides down its side.
Nature's water,
pure and sweet,
bathing its body
in sacred relief.

Time travels on
and so does growth.
Tiny globes
begin to bloom.
Tattooed purple,

bursting with juice,
each bite a blissing,
each flavor proof.

Thirst is quenched
by grape's own gift
fermented, aged,
and gently kissed.
Squeezed from life
into bottled glow,
filling your being
with Earth's soul.

A swirl swiveled in glass
of living memory
nectar born
from sacred history.
The vine's evolution,
without blood or blade
just truth,
unfolding in life's parade.

Through the cycles
of life and death,
we learn what it means
to truly live
with purpose,
with peace,
and with a dance
between give and take.

Hearing The Call

Do you hear that?
A voice rings out
a cosmic phone
through your inner ear,
whispering joy,
laced with success,
as excitement drawing near.

The divine messengers
are breaking through
showing face
in the signs you view.
Synchronicities start to align,
when numbers multiply
crafting sacred rhymes.

Can you hear them now?
They're raising their voices
calling your soul
to conscious choices.
Connect your antennas
through the gaze of intuition.
See the unseen
Isn't that a premonition?

The phone has been ringing.
But you haven't picked up.
What more do you need?
Why stall? Why run?

The signs are clear.
We're reaching out
to lift you through
clouded doubts.

Don't fear the unknown.
That's where growth sprouts
in everyday whispers
you're still figuring out.
Some ties should've been left undone
Loose ends and pain
don't make you strong.
Letting go does.

Surrender the weight
from your shoulder blades.
Your mission's waiting
through the chaos and shade.

Your gifts are buried
in the dirt of pressure.
Dig beneath the surface
and *reclaim your divine essence.*
Remain present with self,
share your art,
ignite the truth
living in your heart.

It's never too late.
Pick up the call.
Let your mindset shift
let fear trust fall.

Divine is calling you back.
By the way
it's your higher self.
Can we have lunch?
We've got so much
to discuss
in the realm of thoughts.

Return of the Gods

Time molded itself
Within the remembered souls
Transformed wombed beings

Breath Taking

A breeze whistled through my lungs,
a sweet taste of freshness
with lavender's scent
easing tension from my body
floating through the summer sky.

There lies an ocean,
off in the distance,
its clear shores stretch wide
across the horizon
with a breeze
brushing my hair
as the wind whistles.

Waves wash the sand's dense body,
rolling beneath subtle winds.
Rocks form a border,
shielding the sea creatures
from reaching the shore.

A whirlpool of water
massages my feet with gentle hands,
cleansing old energies
grounding me fully
in the present moment.

What a time to be alive.
Adrift in wonder,
attuned to the world,
its rhythm grasped
in the palm of my hand.

Can you feel the breeze
flowing through loose clothes,
drying the ocean's kiss

after swimming
in her healing waters?

Rediscovered

Dad Got Your Back

How could a teacher cross that line?
Hands on my son—
like the system ain't already heavy enough
on small shoulders.
Then they hid,
tucked behind metal detectors and silence,
thinking truth don't echo in the halls.

I had words waiting—
don't mistake my quiet for servitude.
You'll hear me coming
like thunder rolling through a valley,
each step clapping the floor
a warning,
a storm brewing.

Distractions rolled 7 or 11 on tables—
noise, excuses, witty
all that polished gibberish.
But I saw through it.
My vision was steady,
locked on justice,
anchored on protecting mine.

The principal tried to corner my son,
her tongue sharp as rusted razors,
digging for confession
where innocence lived.
I pulled him close,
stood eye-to-eye with her hollow vessel,
and let silence erupt truth into the room.

That's when the color bleed,
blue veins trembling over a desk,
her gaze ducking—

not because of me,
but because God's eyes were heavy
in that moment.

I saw the lies stitched
into the seams of her blouse,
threaded bold
but unraveling in my presence.
She thought she had the last word
until I gathered my son
and we walked out,
heads tilted skyward
not broken,
but crowned.

That institution felt like a graveyard,
a cemetery dressed in brick and policy entrapment.
Never again will we bury his light there.
Spells lifted, hexes drowned

Truth rang in my chest
like a phone on fire,
Intuition buzzed loud.
Her story cracked—
so I severed the chains
she tried to seal around my son.

Now he freely explores.
His spirit exhales deeply.
No hands will ever touch him that way again.
When karma circles back,
and justice comes collecting like a grim reaper,
they'll find there's no escape,
no place to repent.

This is the transition of a broken system
but I refuse to let it suppress him.

So I built a stronger foundation,
with rhythm and flow,
a journey where truth can tango.
Homeschool became our adventure,
our way of saying:
Dad got your back.

Brotherly Love

It started out rocky
fights over lifetimes.
From a young seedling
to a harvested potato.

From the start,
you had the upper hand.
Like Scorpion and Sub Zero
jabbing at each other's faces.
Except,
It was thunder-striking trees.

I lost count how many times I dropped
like a fly to a swatter,
a log to a chainsaw.
thirsty for more
hoping to even the score.

I carried you over my shoulder.
Striking me with thunder
I offered you to the ground.
Is that coffee table still around?

It was your shadow drifting,
not mine.
Out flew the curse words.
I calmed your storm
with my mental,
collapsing your dome.

There were moments
outside of Iron Fist tournaments.
Like when you brought me shoes,
or gave me solid advice.
I appreciated the kind gestures.
You oversaw my protection.

You told a lot of truths
through the slurs of your pain.
Liquor drank your breath.
Then came the stories again.

I listened
as you spewed out toxins,
but I never judged you
even in the middle
of crowded fountains.

When you apologized,
I knew reality had knocked you down.
Sit down.
I still want to listen.
Your healing became
your daily mission.

We stretched out our bond,
kneaded bread together.
Visits became frequent.
Look! The wall is patched up.
I always knew that hole was temporary.

That edge-up you gave me?
Felt like Earth and Air synchronizing.
My reflection almost cried.
Those connections
were long overdue.
You even changed my perspective.

You only wanted the best
for your baby brother.
Like a mentor
deconstructing your mind
to feed it the fertilizer of life.

I even forgave you
for cursing out my wife.

We were always close.
We had a weird way
of showing love.
But above all,
I appreciate the daps
and hugs.

You taught me
to keep my head on a swivel,
calculate my moves
before I make them.

That's all I wanted
when I was a young buck
to be just like you.
But life had another thought.

I'm glad I could be of service.
When a phone call
wanders the skies,
we talk for hours
as the days dusk away.

Whenever you need me
I'm just one call away.
Even when egos clash,
and voices erupt from passion

When will this battle ever end?
One of us
has to grow up
to bring this lifelong clash
to its closing credits.

Darkest Hours

Through the depths of my soul,
there is a child unfulfilled.
Afraid to escape the shadows
clouding his path,
suffering in the corner of silence.

He uncovers his eyes
with rain-showers of tears,
begging to see the light again.
Darkness syphon his weakness
his strength, slowly fading away.

In the distance,
a ball of light spins.
but fear keeps him taped
to the floor
of his mind's mysteries.

Curious, he lifts his right hand,
sways his fingers through the haze.
The smoke thins
Reforms thicker.
Stealing his breath away.

Panting for air,
he crawls toward the light
confused by the shifting distance,
squinting his eyes
as the mist tightens like a knot.

He presses forward.
The light morphs
now spread wider,
still visible,
a flicker in the fog.

The fortress binds him
to his knees.
Pressure stiffens the joints
from pressed floor panels
But his legs feel alive again.
With growing strength he rises.
Momentum constructs
his motion.

A hand appears
reaching out.
His fingertips, blackened
just beyond his grip.
By smog and sorrow.

Still,
his breath deepens.
His heartbeat breaks
through the barrier
of slow, sorrowful rhythms.
Inhales rebuild the lungs
of his fading temple.

A muffled voice rings
in the drums of his ears
beating life
back into his weary frame.

The light draws near.
Contrast meets contrast
the zero point,
the threshold,
where stillness meets becoming.

Then, two hands
lift his fainted body
from the hollow ground,

wrap him in a warmth
he thought he'd lost forever.

As the blur lifts from his eyes,
he sees a bearded man
with hair reaching toward the sun,
limbs strong as oak and thunder.
The strength of bulls
and a softness in his smile.

He rubs the crust
from his vision,
and the man smiles wide,
cheek to cheek.
His hug transfers energy
back into the soul-space
the dark tried to steal.

Then the man speaks:
Do you know who I am?
No, the boy replies.
Curiosity outshines the eclipse of his mind.

Then God speaks through the man,
Don't worry, my young friend.
Life gifted you vision
through the buried treasures
of your dreams.

And the man adds,
I am you from the future.
I've come with a message:
Transcend beyond
your hurt and stuggles.
Even in the chaos,
a new version of us is born.

You still have a journey
before you arrive
where I stand now.
But remember to give yourself grace
and express gratitude
for all that you have.

Go forth.
Live out your dreams.
Remember these words:
You are where you need to be.
Be patient
and witness your seeds blossom.

I am you.
And you are me.
We coexist at the same time
separated only by timelines and possibilities.
This version of me
is your higher self
the light you projected
through thought-made-form.
That's when, present
high fived the future.

Breathe

Pause for a moment.
Maybe even five.
You owe it to yourself.
Taking in air is divine.

Inhale deep.
Feel it in your spine.
Exhale slowly
See?
Give it another try.

What thoughts came to the surface?
It's fine to wonder.
Sit down for a moment
We just stepped into summer.

Is stress holding you down?
Let's circle back to that.
As a matter of fact,
There's meditation for that.

Go to a quiet room.
Sit on the floor.
If you're traveling
turn down the music,
but keep your eyes
on the road.

Sit quiet like a toad.
Put a cushion on your bum.
Bring your hands together
make contact with your thumbs.

You've made it this far.
Let's breathe some more.

One more time.
Released what dont belong

Breathe in life.
Exhale stress.
Envision the cold
leaving your chest.

Straighten your spine.
Align your back to the wall.
You can do this seated
cross-legged,
balanced,
tall.

Now imagine a river
with a basket
floating toward the shore.
Grab the notepad.
Write down
what's on your mind.

Put it in the basket.
Let it drift down the river.
Return to yourself.
Let your focus deliver
you home to self.

Focus your attention
between your eyes.
Don't drain
that only leads to pain.
Don't you owe softness
to your brain?

Relax.
Let your mind wander.
Whatever comes,

let it plunder.
You might even start seeing colors
that's your chakras
coming into wonder.

By now,
you've reached the end.
Of this session, at least.
Express gratitude.
Breathe before you release.

I hope this meditation
gave you some relief.
Practice often.
It keeps your mind
from falling.

A little time
is all you need.
Gradually,
increase the time.

Grab a foam roller.
Let it cradle your spine.
All in the name of the divinity
within you.

Who Am I?

Who am I?
God, personified in the flesh.
Was I manifested?
Yes.
Is my skin copper
or stardust blended together?

Who am I?
Mercury mind.
Leo's empowerment.
An Aries lover.
My moon sign?
Represents my mother.

Who am I?
The greatest force
the universe has ever seen.
A magnificent magician
wands from a chariot.
Did my ancestors bury it?

Who am I?
That's for *me* to decide.
Life took me for a ride
roller coaster dives
all the ingredients
of someone divine.

Who am I?
My Higher Self.
My father's secret weapon.
My mother's guardian.
My family's protector.
My sons' Super Heru.

Who am I?
A seed of nature.
The sun's sun.
The moon's light.

Who am I?
I am everything
and everything is me.
One with all life in nature.
This is my destiny.
Thus it shall be

Unknown Awaits

Fear stood on a pedestal,
engulfing flames of terror.
My heart burned its passion away
defeat blocked every error.

He overstood the commitment I lacked.
Tripping over tomorrow's track.
Shoes laced tight around pain's delay.
Bleeding grapes from bones
too tired to pray.
Can this intense ache fade away?

Then
Unknown knocked at my door,
with a message for Fear
a duel by the third eye's stare.

Fear drew the 5 of Swords.
Temperance blocked Unknown's chest.
Every slash collapsed crumbling walls
but she curved a Sun toward Fear's breast.
The reflection
buried his darkness.

The end grew near.
showers of sorrow came trembling down.
Fields blushed with rose-colored moons.
Dawn broke through devil's battleground
shattering chains to birth renewed stars.

It was too much for Fear to bear.
So he withdrew
from the sacred square.
Saddled his shadow,
disappeared through
the forest of light.

Bright futures unfolded
in divine timing.

Libra casted judgment that day.
Temperance's shield
laid on the castle floor.
Unknown claimed victory
in uncharted terrain.
What new adventures await
behind every door?

With each step
into Unknown's fortress.
visions of life
rise before me,
and waiting to be explored.

We Are One

Double the trouble
Masculine and Feminine
The dance of twin flames

The ABC's of Life

A is for *attention* to your dreams.
B, *believe in self* — no in-between.

C is *choose to attract, not chase.*
D is *drive* — keep a steady pace.

E for *elevation* as you tour your path.
F for *finding purpose* that will last.

G is *gathering all the tools you need.*
H, *higher heights* — you're born to lead.

I is *inner wisdom*, let it grow.
J for *jumping for joy* as you glow.

K, *keep momentum*, let it build.
L are the *levels* you climb with skill.

M for *mountains*, tall and steep.
N, *never quit*, just dig in deep.

O, *open mind* to what can be.
P, *push past fear* to be truly free.

Q for *quiet nights of rest.*
R, *righteous choices* manifest.

S says *don't settle*, raise the bar.
T for *testing limits* near and far.

U is *understanding what you need.*
V, *variety*, to plant your seed.

W, *win* each time you try.
X for a *xenial* essence that made you cry.

Y — *you made it*, now take it in.
Z — *the zone* where you always win.

You *navigated these ABC's* with grind and grace
Because you honored the path, and ran your race

Grounded

Did you know trees
have a root system
growing like grapevines
beneath the soil
of Mother Earth

A little seedling
born into the dirt,
connected to an underground
communication center
older than any internet.

Look at your hair?
See how it grows?
Your body is the tree trunk.
Your feet
are the roots.
When they touch the ground,
energy dispels,
flows,
and releases.

The water you drink
feeds your inner organs.
The food you eat
fertilizes your cells.

The breath of life
travels like branches
through darkness,
while the outer shell
receives the light.

When I gaze at the sun,
I see hues of red,
yellow,

and orange
with a green aura.
That's what stuns my eyes.
As if the sun
sends secret codes
straight through my crown.

My retina births
sights of vibrating color
sorting through the library
of incoming energy,
like a rainbow
after summer's rain.

The geometry
of this physical construct
it speaks
if you sit still enough
to listen.

At the beach
the waves pick up your pain,
toss it into the ocean,
to replenish you.

Your feet
release negative charge
into the pool of sand
beneath you.

Or maybe you're laying
on a yoga mat
at spring's peak
or in summer's heat,
dancing to nature's rhythm
while her heartbeat
plays beneath your spine.

A cosmic dance
with your inner garden
moving mountains,
breaking boulders,
releasing tension
from your shoulders.

Cobra pose
to realign the back,
as the chakras
sing softly in tune.

Something so simple
as soil
can erase
the ache you've buried.
It helps the brain
flow with deeper passions
not masked in sorrow.

We borrow
others' energy
just by revisiting
the story of trauma.
But can we
just let it go?
Can we stop
recycling the drama?

Nature's medicine
is only a backyard away.
Even the beach
calls you to its breath
to lay inside
its dreamy waters.

Take a moment.
Bask in the power.
Let your body
revitalize
in nature's shower.

Breathe life
into your inner waters
alchemize
its sacred patterns.
Restructure your matter
so your thoughts
can gather.
So your mind
won't feel
scattered.

Sacrifices

What have you sacrificed?
The dreams you carried for years
just to satisfy
your vampire peers,
leeching off your energy field,
draining you
of your individuality
just so *they*
can shape your reality.

They feared you leaving.
So they held tight to old memories
wanting to relive
scenes of perished feelings.
Do they even know
the new you?

When you journeyed on,
they gossiped and preached
speaking your downfall
into existence.
As if moving on was a curse.

Would you leave those people behind?
The ones that gripped your spine,
stripped you of all that's divine?
Why stay compressed
by what only gave you stress?

What about your ego?
The thoughts that ran miles ahead
Even when you smiled,
you still couldn't get ahead.
Your motivation bled dry,
left for dead,

as the voices echoed
inside your head.

When will you leave it alone?
The phone's been ringing
with opportunities.
But every time you picked up,
voicemails flooded in
like a bill collector
asking when you'd pay
your potential.

So you imprisoned your ideas
next to the drive
for arraignment.

Who really held you back?
Was it fearful people
avoiding the leap.
Or you,
thinking too hard
with cold feet.

Defeated
by voices screaming:
You'll never be enough.

What if you sacrificed
other people's opinions
in exchange for your road to winning.
Supercharged
by your new beginning,
leaping with faith
on the other line.
Can you paint the picture?

Then you fainted.
You'd had enough.

The friction
started within.

Now it's time
to tighten up.
Break the fear.
Release the tears.
Let passion deliver
it's final blow.

Your wealth begins
when you lighten the load.
You're heavier than Tyson's punch
but the feathers of heaven
now rest
on the gut of a lion's soul.
Courage woke
from its mighty rut.

Listen to your
heartbeat rumble.
Don't let a linebacker's dream
make you fumble.
Strap up your gloves,
get ready to rumble.

Hold your head high.
Stay focused.
Pause before you stumble.
And remember
to be humble.

Gratitude will carry you
through rain and thunder.
Don't fall back
into Past's sleepy slumber.

Champions are made
in the silence of night
when you ride life's waves
with your first eye's sight.

Compassion

I am thankful
for the good times and the bad
singing in the shower
whispering songs and humming melodies,
as the healing waters wash away
pain remembered through vision cells .

I am grateful
to my friends and family
checking on me,
sending uplifting messages,
providing comfort
through my rough patches.

I express compassion
for the food that feeds me
fueling my cells,
satisfying my cravings,
strengthening my muscles,
supercharging my manifestations.

Every bite fulfills
my taste buds
and nourishes
my mind, body, and spirit.

Compassion is gratitude,
expressed in motion.
It's the honoring
of all that I have
while welcoming more

holding space
for the new
to parade in
like the ten of pentacles,

riding the whistling winds
of change.

Gratitude to my brother Pete
for yoga flows
that realign my chakras,
for meditations
that welcomed clarity,
and for closing each session
with words of gratitude
to jumpstart
this renewed energy cycle.

Pushing Through

Get out of bed.
Shame's sweating you.
You lost yesterday
but that was the passing
of old worries.
Today's got new victories waiting.

Dodge the fear-mongering.
Slap social media out.
End calls soaked in gossip.
Take the long road home
Avoid the traffic and chaos.
Allow your soul to detour the path.

Give yourself grace.
Pace yourself.
This is your race.
Competition?
It breeds separation
from purpose.

Prep for the long haul
late night gym visits,
magnesium for sore muscles,
amino acids to build strength,
and water to baptize
the body in movement.
Sweat escapes
the grip of yesterday's weight.

Keep going
you got it.
Feel the pain
then push through it
by doing it *again.*
Increase the reps

when the hurt stops hurting.
Isn't that how muscles grow?

That business idea?
It never left the ground.
Pick the ball back up.
You missed some shots
but the fog is clearing.
Your groove is returning.
Now you're hitting from half court.

Stay level-headed.
Lead with gratitude
and quiet strength
the kind that overcomes pitfalls.
Isn't this what you prayed for?

Pick yourself up.
Rise beyond the shadow
of what didn't work.
Reshape your mind.
Unravel within your passions.
Journal your discoveries
as they unfold.

This path?
It's preparing you
For everlasting joy.
So nurture it
Embody it
and become it.
Embrace your purpose

Legacy Builder

What impact will you leave
when you transcend this reality?
Will you uplift the people
or will your name
be etched in shame.
What direction
are you directing?

You are the star
of this movie
life continues to televise
projected through the lens
of your mind,
guided by the sight
of your first eye.
Will you speak your existence
into reality?

Will people remember you
for the help you gave,
or the back-stabbing
where the streets
were paved with bodies,
and guilt was written
in footprint signatures.

Did you watch your movie play out
in your imagination?
Dreaming at night
about how you could've made it.
As if effort
j-walked into your life.

Could you have made it?
You witnessed peer pressure
from devils who drank poison,

127

the stench of spirits
coughed out
by tongues numb to truth.

Why would you sell yourself short?
when the world of life
waits to embrace you.
The wind brushes your skin
like an energetic kiss
filling your body
with passions
your heart can't resist.

Legacy starts
By embodying the light spectrum
in a creative expression.
When you choose
to embrace all parts
the dark and the light.
When you marry
the many masks of you.

Balance becomes your compass.
Let the scales of Ma'at
tip in your favor.
Can you taste the wine
drained from the grapes
you cast-iron pressed
juices of endeavor,
now pouring truth into your cup.
What will you be known for?
Can you keep pace
with your own calling?

How will it look on you?
Will you wear it
like a jacket of smiles,

sneakers laced with grace,
a crown of ideas
orbiting your mind.

Message to the Patriarch

FREEZE!
You're surrounded,
As if I'd ever subscribe
to your patriarchal disease
A system rooted
in breaking down families,
built on falsehoods
and broken realities.
We ain't standing on that.

You paper-signing,
land mass stealing,
Harry and Paul–faced ass,
pistol-toting,
pig-of-a-heart having,
insecure ass,
wannabe us
but you can't, lookin' ass.

Be yourself, for once.
You'll never be us.
Direct your threats
to those who gives a fuck
about your non rhythm having
unorthodox ways of living.

Talk about church-going
but you the one sinning.
You should be the jail's sentence
Welcome to hell, bitches.
Call the witness to the stand
I bet that nigga still missing.

You can't dot an I
when your T's ain't crossing.

Wasting time
building prisons
while you being played
by some alien wishes.

Time's up.
Pack your bags.
Slow-walk the plank.
Grow a pair
pods still missing peas,

Stop playing "GOD"
when your shit's fictitious.
The contract reads
GONE.
OVER.
DONE.

Your plane has arrived
but it's a one-way ticket
to your mental prison.

Hate don't look good on you
uglier than your sense of style.
Orthopedic shoe-wearing'
Feet never catch a charge,
the ground hates
the touch of your soles.

The planet's shifting.
She awakened from her slumber.
And so did her original inhabitants.
Her roots remembered.

The underground won't save you.
Karma's got lungs
and she wants all the smoke.

This is your final move.
Checkmate!
All across the board.
While burning your britches.
That's a hot-shit fall
with a dumpster-themed toilet
wipe your ass with the smog.

And when you wake up?
It won't be heaven
Just a:
Never.
Ending.
Fall.

Sincerely,
The Upper Room.

Socially Distant

What has the world come to?
The most dangerous disease
left us home to wonder:
How many thieves rest under these masks?
There's a cover-up operation.
Was this a premonition from my mother?

Mom foretold visions of destruction and chaos.
It frightened me at first, but rested in my mental.
You had to be higher than school
to see that picture.
But what did her message really mean?

2020 began with a crowned jewel,
discovered in a crash
that aired on a cartoon.
What are the odds of that?

They had to tell us
before the news.
Broken hearts pitied the fool.

I never knew
how silly humans could be
until I saw one
walking their dog
outside
with a mask on.

Did they forget
They were outdoors?
Lack of oxygen
must've gotten to them.

Since when did wearing masks
become law?

Or was this a policy
enforced by magicians
hiding behind stage curtains?

Have you seen The Wizard of Oz?
I was in awe
watching people fall
for wicked tales
packaged as lies and fraud.

Heavy metal-ridden bodies,
walking in dis-ease.
Can't think straight,
'cause the hot-sauced arm pokes
erased the common sense
they had left.
Can you piece together
the rest of this mess?

Take a moment to breathe.
Some couldn't resist
but were judged by controlled pawns
stacked on offense.
Ain't no checkmate
over here.

Checkerboarded minds
couldn't wait to get back outside.
There was too much
they'd missed.
The media frenzy
had people reaching.
just to be dismissed
from the prison
of social distance.

Intuition and logic
played on the bench.
While zombies huddled,
mumbling Stockholm scriptures.
Breaks threw interceptions
on damn near every play.
I bet the coach
read plays from
the Lay-Z-Boy those days.

How could we not see it coming?
Sounds familiar?
Like a script
from the archives.
Originality bled dry.
Even the movies
broadcast the signs.

The true artists
want their lines back
along with their masters
that dug early graves.
Because ownership
is better these days.

Let the record show
through the daze
of mentally strained brains
social distance lifted
but left minds stranded.

The fog
wasn't weather.
It was oppression.
A mental daze.

But the brave
played a tight game.

It ain't over yet.
That was just
the test subjects' intro.
A reality of chance
like a dice game.
Play the cards you were dealt
collect your prize
at the reunion.

As you stargaze
through this reality of chance,
remember:
this world will never be the same.

Don't socially distance yourself
from the game of life.
Just play
your cards
right.

Fallen Bridge

As waters rust away
the metal columns in wave-pool sway,
foundations crumble under pressure
too many travelers,
too much cargo to leverage.

Lane-changers spark collision fate,
road closures choke the interstate.
Wheeled vessels pile in heaps,
oceans shift
but silence keeps.

Why'd we fall so deep beneath
the spells of maritime belief?
Jurisdictions cloaked in code,
military zones where
postcards never go.

Ships dock in ghostly stations,
sailors move with no foundations.
And yet I've never seen before
a bridge collapse
on Baltimore's shore.

A key bridge, gone.
Where commerce flew
now severed veins
of revenue.
A wound upon the harbor's chest,
Eastside groans beneath unrest.

Planned attacks or fate's design?
Surprise wears masks
on borrowed time.
While gossip floods
the talk-show waves,

stillness creeps
through tidal graves.

Mermaids hum
beneath the mist,
tugging at the theorist's twist.
Tunnel vision, shadow cast,
conspiracies no longer last.

The illusion has fallen.
The veil is torn.
The silence hushed
by truth reborn.

Voices lost
for what was spoke,
mysteries wrapped
in heavy smoke.

The masses sleep
while monsters eat
but now we rise
on waking feet.

Their crooked grins
and chattering lies
can no longer blindfold
these seeing eyes.

The bridge has fallen.
So has the spell.
We've risen up
we know too well.
Our one way ticket out of hell.
The mental space

Having The Conversation

Courage stepped forward
Weakness erased from my shoulders,
like a boulder rolled off my back.
My tongue was heavy with truth,
words vibrating like live wires,
ready to spark.

I dialed the third-oldest—
several rings, then a voice.
I proceeded with facts,
dove headfirst into memory's fountain,
the water cold,
the bottom lined with pain.

The humiliation,
company watching
while you nailed me to the floor.
That twist-dial phone,
colliding against my head,
crown split,
scar stitched permanently.
A tattoo of revival.

Funny how spirits and powders
blur the line between temper and delusion.
But I refused to let you
suppress my truth.
These stories breathe—
etched deep in the albums
of my childhood.

And still—
you respected the telling.
That alone lit a spark in me.
I felt the charge surge,

Hand gloved the infinity gauntlet,
stones glowing,
power returning,
though I was still
a few shy of wholeness.

Then came the raging bull.
The fourth-eldest.
Apologies once whispered,
but my pain stayed frozen,
snowflakes locked in ice,
untouched by time unfolding.

At first, the call was calm
smooth waters.
But then my truth separated the sky,
thunder against his martian pride.
He raged.
Armies collided on technology.
Withdrawal followed fast.
He couldn't hold the storm
I gifted to the room.

I extended peace.
He turned his palms away.
So I was left with silence,
unsatisfied,
still searching.

One remained.
Dreams showed me the script.
Vision told me:
This is the moment.
But to you—
It was a comedy.
You laughed at the weight of my truth,
cutting the line mid-sentence.

Bitterness slammed the call shut,
cell phone click sharp as a slap,
acid spitting through static.

Then came the text.
Words hit like fists,
ego shattered
on the glass floor of honesty.
But I stood steady.
I always knew this fire was in me,
time just had to season it.

Now I stand
above leveled ground,
head tilted toward the heavens.
The battlefield behind me,
the scar still throbbing,
but victory was claimed.
Even if the ache lingers,
truth has no silence anymore.
My condolences to the storms.

What If?

What if you ate clean every day?
Would your health problems fade away?

What if you journaled your thoughts?
Would your mind escape through the clouds?

What if you gave yourself more love?
Would the mask finally melt away?

What if you embodied your higher self—
and personified it now?

What if trauma was preparation
for something greater?
A foundation laid
for your ultimate power
morphed like a caterpillar
within 24 hours.
Life transitioned
after the fall of the tower.

What if you gave more attention to your craft?
Divorcing the inner critic
chanting all your wishes
Then people showed up,
pushing you closer
to your purpose at last.

What if the world
hovered in your palm?
You snapped your fingers
and all your dreams appeared.
Your mind tapped into the infinite all
you became the greatest inventor
embraced in your time.

What if you manifested
your wildest dreams?
And life was filled with happiness
while stress became your seventh cousin
twice removed.
You never even knew it existed.

What if your physical reality
is a dream?
And when you slept
the real one began.
Your mind grew strong.
You found the portal
to escape this planet.

What if you walked
in the shoes of your intuition?
Chest moves .
Mistakes became your greatest lessons
and you release
the stronghold of stressing.

What if you took a walk in nature?
The answers became clear
and you heard the voice of God
like a phone call
ringing in your ear.

What if fear
was never a thing?
You stepped out on faith,
trust in yourself,
and gave self
more grace.

What if this is
your current reality?

You took my advice.
Welcome balance.
And your mind
cleared the brain fog.

What if you're already ready
for the next phase of life?
You made the move.
Created healthy habits.
Then life became
your greatest satisfaction.

Have you read this far?
Then you got the message.
What are you waiting for?
You have *always* been
your greatest blissing.

Keep embracing growth.
You've got work to do.
Stay focused.
Remain in motion.

Now you have
the final ingredient.
It was always
YOU.

Gem-in-i

Paradise Island

I longed for a vacation.
Tropical skies lit my eyes
the scent of pineapples and coconut
nurtured my nostrils with delight.

The Sun radiated through stillness.
Fueling my cells,
feeding my crown with light.
The beach swallowed my body whole,
and my mind drifted into paradise.

Pigeons befriended me
in exchange for sugar cookies and chips.
The city could never change my mind
This was the most beautiful sight.

We toured the island,
sipping rich, volcanic coffee
that erupted warmth through my body.
At the soap factory,
nature carried me through its softness.

My Concord 11s hated the dirt.
who cares about Concord's feelings
He could bathe when we get home.

I was just enjoying the vibrancy of the island.
It felt like royalty had scored a touchdown
while my soul kicked the extra point..

There was a resonance in the sand
a reflection of my own energy,
mirrored in the crystal waters.
Trash had no place here today.

Kamehameha
felt like a distant ancestor,
watching me through my tourist spirit
through the sacred realms of ancestral lands.
When will I take three flights again?

Rewind became a distant film
before it wrapped around me
like a blanket over my eyes
I missed a flight.
Still, it was worth it.
Even the lady in first class
speaking volumes of books
couldn't ruin my travels.

I reminisce through visions.
Will I ever go back?
Asked El-Yoshuah.
To be continued...

Feels Like Home Again

The wind wandered through the windows.
Blinds concealed my dirty sins.
The shed laid my passions to rest,
as air exhaled through my chest.

Hinges creaked with unhealed wounds.
Floorboards peeled back old scars.
The furnace coughed trapped breaths,
and the smell lingered room to room.

The aftermath witnessed
tumbled weeds and tall grass.
The lawnmower
empty of gas.
Will this house stay afloat?

The storm passed
after months of distress.
Winter subdued broken limbs,
leaving patches in the flower beds.
Will roses ever bloom again,
filling the air with peace and love?

March kissed Spring's petals,
enriching seedlings breaking ground.
Summer waited
in the shadow of the moon,
while roots reached
above and below.
Water vibrated the atmospheric dome.

Out came the builder
through night's quiet chill
the dark night of the soul's abyss.
His shadow hugged clouds of smog,

while the scent of Egyptian musk
burned through the chimney bricks.

Hammer KO'd nails that day,
paving the roof
through haunted rain.
Snowmelt poisoned the air
lonely trees wept in silence.
At night I had a dream
not even Martin could see.

Dancing in oceans of moonshine,
starch pierced my empty belly.
The moon smiled
through stained glass mosaics
my ancestors
drew closer to me.

As the sun returned,
titans of heat rose.
Bronzed feet soaked in light.
Beneath the winds' surface,
a thousand stories lay
but one man held the key
to his force within.

The destroyer
went into hibernation.
The builder stepped forward
sweeping the house,
breathing life
with holy wood.
The shadow figures
withered away.

Smoke cast a spell
of good fortune.

While misfortune
tuned out the treble.
Michael moonwalked
through my eardrums,
drumming new beginnings
between clotheslines,
as I folded towels
and smelled cologne soaps.

Rust fell asleep.
Oils awakened my hue.
The mirror winked at me
as the stars began to glow.
The rays of the sun
walked with me.

This was the story
of a wounded warrior
and Leo had waited
for this moment
to awaken the sun within.

Home smelled of sweet basil
and lavender.
Cast iron sizzled
on a flat top.
Hearts of palm rested in oil,
frying love into the air
with sautéed broccoli
and walnuts
well-seasoned
until the ancestors said stop.

Garlic-cheesy mashed potatoes
 graced a table
where the family prayed.
Happiness erupted

within our sacred space.
Love pierced
through every forkful,
while alkaline water
cleansed our throats.

The brisk cold sent
chills through my cells
as if there was a house party
in my bones.

We laughed,
jokes to old-school jams,
while the starseeds
danced the floor away.
We sang our love
like a sacred hymn.
It felt like home again.

Love On You

Give yourself more attention
the same way you do
when you're speaking to crowds
or showing up for others.
That love you display?
It deserves to lay on you
like fresh silk sheets
after a warm shower
on a heavy day.

You give so much attention to
phones,
scrolls,
social media,
Netflix shows & movies...
but none
to the inner you.

We invest in intangible assets
but forget to deposit
into the private places
of our being.
Caring for seeds from other beings
leaving us drained,
our spirits restless,
desires depleted.

Instead—
speak on your achievements.
Journal your self-image.
Embody those visions
into your current walk.

Isn't your existence valuable?
Are your feelings being heard?
Do you tend to your inner garden?
Is your vibration expanding?

What color pulses in your aura?

These questions
will echo in your mind
when you're ready to change
to realign your reality
with the visions
future you have lived.

Don't just *believe* in yourself.
Know that you're appreci-loved.
Affirm it.
Speak it.
Feel it.
Express your greatness
in your daily devotions.

Grace has stood before you
patient,
face softened,
waiting for your mind
to hug it
with the warmth of self-care.

You deserve more than
what you've been pouring out.
Start pouring in.
Affirm you Ace of Cups

Visionary

A brilliant mind enhanced,
with grapevine neurons,
electrifying the pulse of thought
raging rivers of affirmation
through the projector of the eyes.

A vision unfolds:
people aligning with your dreams,
merging patterned pieces
to create symphonies.

Floating in the infinite
space of your expanded mind,
the wonders of the universe
reside in your mind's eye.

Creation sees itself
blooming from stomach seeds
to embodied trees,
with curly, coiled hair
and toenail roots reaching deep.

You gaze at sunrise beams
light sending downloads
through your crown's mass,
illuminating the golden jewels:
the precious stones of your mind.

You are earth's living jewel
eternal.
Teleporting through portals
after lifelong journeys,
traveling the galaxies within,
phasing from one dream
into another.

You are the embodiment of God
personified in the flesh.
Monotonic metals
and celestial liquids
flow through your cells,
exploding magic
from your fingertips.

The first wand was your hand.
And beside you,
the wombman
the portal of life,
birthing form
from the manifestation of man's soldiers,
marching to fertilize
the golden egg.

Your first home
was formed in darkness
body extending
from brain and spine seedling,
until you bloomed
into the essence of a garden.

A seed sprouted.
Nerves and cells aligned,
baking in the fertile ground
of your mother's womb
until you pushed forth
from her sacred tomb.

A portrait of her light
made into the image
of a young god
wise beyond years,
housed with ancestral knowledge.

You came back
to make a difference.
Now, complete the mission.

Motivation

Knock. Knock.
Who's there?
Motivation.
Not today, my friend.

You can't run from me.
Sit down, let's have a little chit chat.
This time, you might even get
a pat on the back.

Don't be swallowed by the chair.
Relax.
Take a wholesome breath.

I know there's weight on your chest
worried about running away
when it felt like no one had your back.
Your subconscious was gossiping again
giving free piggybacks.

That's a fact.
You're overwhelmed with life
but don't forget,
you created this experience.

Change flows through your spine.
When you were born,
it was nothing short of divine.
And when you look in the mirror
don't forget to smile.

Rainy days come
when time runs away.
But *this* is the motivation today:

Get up. Get out. Feel the sun's rays.
Take a walk with the kiddos.

You've always hit the mark
until thoughts raced marathons.
Be one with the flows in life.
Yes, I know you lost your first wife.
But take a chill for a second
Everything will be alright.

This isn't a battle.
This isn't a fight.
You might just need to exercise
pull out that bike.

A running mind
sat your body down.
Open your playlist.
Jam to your favorite sound.

Stress won't take you anywhere.
So continue to show up for *you*.
No more hiding
behind that invisible shelf.

Book a massage.
Roll the windows down.
Let the wind sing to your thoughts.
Breathe the outcome into existence.
Just flow without resistance

Practice yoga as a sacred art.
Your body will thank you later.
And don't be fooled
by your imagination.
Follow your intuition.

You've come a long way.
Don't give in to frustration
unless you want a dinner date
with your health.
That kind of meal robs wealth.
Remember:
Knowledge of self.

Express how you feel
even if no one's listening.
Get in the mirror.
Speak your vision.

Reminder:
Clean the dishes.
Use lavender.
Calm the mind.
It'll be okay.
Give healing
a little time.

This is a gamble worth taking.
The results?
Not distant.
In fact
they're in your grasp.

Be patient.
Be *you* to the fullest.
Isn't that what you are?
And when life gets tough,
remember this poem.

There is a quiet before the storm.
Listen closely
the winds are whispering.

There's nothing to catch
when free will is your breast plate.
Get plenty of rest.
Follow your script to be your best.
Let life show you the rest.

This talk has been divine .
I hope to see you soon
but next time,
let it be to document your progress.
By the time I return
stress will have dissolved.

Back to the universe I go.
Journal your journey.
It'll be your best friend
the gift that keeps unwrapping.
Let the pen relieve your stress.
No more messages for the day.
Your body imprinted the rest.

I Love You.
To the stars and betyond.
Twice infinity squared.
And no take backs.

← *Motivation has left the chat.*

We Are

We are smart.
We are intelligent.
We are handsome or beautiful.
We are brave.
We are strong.
We are powerful.
We are amazing.
We are everything

and everything is us.

We are one with all life in nature.

We are the greatest forces in the universe.

That which We are

and so much more.

And don't ever forget that.

Repeat this to yourself and the kiddos in the rising,
before rest at night, or anytime throughout the energy cycle.
Let the words be felt, not just spoken.
Let them become your tribe's daily rhythm.

Affirmations For Self-Growth

I honor myself daily,
and my visions reveal themselves with clarity.

Each day, I peel away doubt
and embrace the fullness of my genius.

My cells vibrate with joy,
gratitude, love, abundance, prosperity,
and all things divine.

My mind is clear,
and my presence is felt
in every room I step into.

I am divinely guided, guarded,
and protected by my ancestors.

I attract people, places, and opportunities
that serve my journey and support my highest good.

I love and appreciate myself deeply,
and I affirm it daily.

I speak and write my wildest dreams
into existence with purpose and power.

I feel the essence of God
flowing through every part of my being.

I am the embodiment of my highest self.

Use these affirmations during your rising rituals, mirror work, or moments of self-alignment.
They are seeds for expansion, breath for becoming, and a reflection of who you truly are.

What's Your Purpose

When a table sits still
on a shiny wood floor,
doesn't it laugh
at the dishes it holds,
while chairs pull up
beneath its belly
on wandering feet.

Then laughter erupts
from the screws in its spine,
holding its legs
and platform in line
as the smell of savory food
Send clouds through the ethers,
warming the room
like a memory had.
It knows its purpose.
It doesn't complain.

Then come the dishes,
shiny as polished leather,
waiting to be dirtied
by the food the table's seen.
But this time,
they lock in.
A front row seat
to the seasoned host.

Forks play music
a DJ on turntables,
spinning across porcelain
like legends in fables.
Finger swipes,
tongue licks,

graceful spins and clinks
But do they complain?

Look at the fork and spoon
in harmony they dance,
taking turns around the ferris wheel
of the plate's round glance,
divinely led
into the mouths
of living beings.
Yet they never
quit their jobs.

Take a look
at the *living being*—
You.
with so many gifts
woven through your essence.

A mind beyond this world,
navigating the physical,
feeling life's rhythm
in and out of form,
called to fulfill
a heart's pure purpose
before the sun grows warm.

Did you give up on your mission?
I doubt that you did.
You came through a portal
from sacred waters
carried through
your mother's womb
to make a change

You are your ancestors'
wildest dreams
the walking legacy
of divine extremes.
You are here
to carry the fire,
to spread God's gifts,
to climb ever higher.

So what's your purpose?
The world still waits.
Pull up your seat
and fill your plate.

Missing Link

The cord of my spine
Rest within the bounds of my
Soul's purpose visions

Forever and Always

I'm grateful for your presence
matter of fact, your entire existence.
You taught me so much.
Let me tell you the rest.

You provided like no other.
You barely got any rest.
Aries poked out your chest
you are God personified in the flesh.

Your foundation is a monument.
Your words could shatter windows.
Your work ethic? Invincible.
What couldn't you do?

Grocery store runs to Giants were the best.
We always grabbed donuts as a snack,
with sparkling water piercing our lungs.
Those Grand Marquis rides? Timeless.

Solar returns were a celebration
Chuck E. Cheese, Golden Corral
Gifts opened up my heart.
But really it was always just the thought.

In 2003. A game changer.
I hated seeing you weakened.
I ran out of that hospital.
Rite Aid became my safe space.

Mom was mad that I ran
but when she looked at me,
she innerstood.
I wasn't just scared.
I was hurting with you.
As if *your pain* was *my body.*

You had to relearn life all over again
writing with your left,
dragging your legs,
leaning on that cane
until will became your shield.

It blanketed your emotions,
but didn't stop your momentum.
You walked daily.
Sometimes, I joined you.
When you were gone,
your presence remained.

Kisses on the forehead kept me strong.
So did your will to keep going.
What a beautiful soul.
God gave me a warrior dad,
always armoured for challenges.
Your motivation whispers in my thoughts.

Remember fixing the Trooper?
That door kicked *both* our asses.
Even with the wrong hinges
We made it work.
If only help came sooner that day.

But we laughed anyway.
Westerns brought us together,
so did Sunday Night Football.
Remembered in my mental projector.

You taught me how to be a man.
Your advice filled my spirit.
My ears *tickled* to hear your wisdom.
There was never a dull moment
in this earthly experience.

I remember
I hated you once
for being disciplined.
But you were teaching me
how to listen,
how to learn.
I was just being stubborn.
I didn't make those mistakes again.

So let's create more memories.
Build your favorite car.
Catch a drag race.
Or maybe just talk
long conversations, no rush.
The possibilities are endless.
We'll figure something out.

I still yearn for your hugs
followed by *Always*
every time we part.
I came back for one more hug.
Because you're the best father in the world

Forever and Always.

Earth's Angel

I wonder what you've been up to lately.
It's been a while.
I glamour over pictures
especially the ones where you smiled.

You've shown up in many dreams.
I feel your presence,
your quiet protection.
You played the background
while the energy permeated.

You were gold before form.
Kids flowed to you easily.
Your love was tremendous.
Even while you're gone
I still feel it.

I can still taste your fried salmon cakes,
with a side of whole cake bread.
Mac and cheese with tomatoes
that hint of sweetness was always there.

Fried soft-shell crabs,
pressed between two slices of bread.
And I'll never forget when you taught me
how to crack an egg.
I remember how breakfast
weighed down my fork.

Gold crafted your heart
precious to its touch.
Your love immersed
everything it touched.

When Dad got sick,
I could tell it was too much.

But like him,
your warrior shined on the surface.
Even when emotions were masked,
your smile was a reminder
a daily dose of devotion,
wrapped in rain.

I wonder why you suffered in silence.
*How did you hold it all in
and it never turned violent?*
I guess you just knew how
better than most.

You spoke truths
that pinned egos to the wall.
You knew the world was going to end.
You told everyone: *don't be afraid.*

Beauty whispered from your tongue.
You could tell a story
better than anyone could write.
You were misunderstood at times
but I always felt
like I was the one who *got it.*

I wish I could've had more hugs.
The troubled one stole your attention.
He needed it more than some.
And each time he slipped
you never left his defense.

I wonder if the words in your mind
ever uttered:
Why is he attracted to trouble?

You were the half that kept him whole
until your transition
to the ancestral realm.

And only then
did he finally divorce trouble.

But you already knew not to worry.
Because strength lingered
in the light you left behind.

I miss you
more than words can explain.
I can't wait to dream of you again.

In one dream,
you wore a red dress.
I hold that image
close to my chest.

I often wonder:
How were you so strong?
You were built from the earth's crust,
with waterfalls of love,
and a hint of *"tell it like it was."*
You were one of
my favorite Psalms.

Say hello to Jade for me.
You still protect me in your silence
a mother's love never leaves.
I still feel you in the quiet moments
when I forget to be strong.

Queen of Cups

From the moment we met,
I saw a glimpse of my life
and there you were,
pasted in the vision
like you'd always been there.

You welcomed me in
like a son you'd always known
not just the man
dating your eldest daughter,
but family,
flesh of heart.

You called me son
and that word stitched
a smile across my chest,
a warmth rising
like sunrise through ribs.

You always knew
how to lift my spirit
without crushing my feelings.
Our laughter filled rooms,
echoed off ceilings.
Tiredness tried to interrupt
but joy kept taking the mic.

Comedy lived in the living room
as we performed sacred improv
you, the anchor
with humor and grace.

It feels good
to be mothered again
to receive advice
that heals

without judgment,
to be seen
without being fixed.

You are everything I asked for
a mother who stepped up
after mine ascended
to the ancestral realm.
She knew I'd still need
a mother's love in the flesh,
and the universe
sent you as her echo.

I light up when you call.
We reminisce,
make sense of now,
and dream forward
into forever.

Love you, Mom.
I'll honor your heart's wishes
wrap your joy in hugs and kisses,
and give back the love
you so freely give.

Cheers to July

Summer kissed your eyes
Copper never looked so good
Is that love I see?

On a 5 day

How more aligned could it have been?
It was the afternoon of the 18th.
Whole Foods was the in-between.
I saw you in that black dress.

Your hair was long and black,
falling halfway down your back.
I saw how shy you were.
I felt your energy
through your clothes.

Then we took the kiddos to the park
not too far away.
That moment alone
made my day.

An oracle crossed our path
I think she was a divine witness.

We created an energetic bond.
Even the bench
seemed to stretch and grow.
The sun shined brightest where we sat
as if he was listening
to our conversation.

I bet
he told the universe
what happened.

Let's go back to the beginning...

There was harmony in our minds.
I crossed your path a second time.
I just knew

this was all divine.
I'll always keep that in mind.

You were the perfect copper tone.
Your nose, beautifully shaped
resembling stars.
Legs, uniquely made
The shine
blinded me at first sight.

It feels so right.
In every reality,
I see you in it.
No other divine feminine.

We danced in flower fields
tulips, roses, lavender.
White was the occasion.
Our inner childs were present.

A preview
to a long, loving life.
I will one day
make you my wife.
Side by side,
we grow together
no more storms
we have to weather.

Tis' the season for destiny.
She made herself known
in the presence of love.
Cancer reminded us
of who we are.

July treated us so well.
Cheers to love and light.
This was both our second chance.

The future
is bold and bright.

Love Notes

KNOCK! KNOCK!
Who's there?
You.
You who?

You are amazing.
You are beautiful.
You are bold.
You are fierce.
You are excellence.
You are greatness.

You are loved.
You are cared for.
You are divine.
You are protected.
You are loving.
You are caring.

You are everything
I've been looking for.
You are my manifestation
manifested.

I love you, baby.

P.S. — You look so amazing
in that olive green dress
especially with that long, curly natural hair.
Can I see that again,
and again,
and again?

Use What You Have

Use what you have.
The resources that flow
through your infinite thought patterns
ready to exist
once pulled from the mental realm
into form.

The portal of your mind
exists beyond language.
Words can't truly name it
but your physical actions
give it voice.
They make it make sense.

Through your:
spoken spells,
written agreements,
divine intuition,
energetic hands,
and root-like feet
planted into Earth's belly

You are the motherboard
of your own reality
a living CPU
that channels creation
through organic code,
housed in a god-body
that magically magicians your life
into motion.

Go make the impossible possible.
Defy the odds.
Move against the grain.
Make your ancestors proud.

Your higher self
is waiting at the next checkpoint
baton in hand,
ready for the handoff
so you can finish
what you came here to complete.

And when you do
you'll leave the blueprint behind
for the seedlings
that sprout
into your family tree.

Gem-in-i

I see the gem in you.
Do you see the Gem-in-I?
I see the gem will shine
Let that river cry.

When you start living in truth,
and stop living a lie
that's when you hear the cry
of the Gem-in-I.

I see the gem in you
Do you see the Gem-in-I?
I see the gem can shine
Let those rivers cry.

When you start living *your* truth,
and stop living a lie,
you'll see the gem in you
that's the Gem-in-I.

I've cried a thousand times
because I was living a lie.
But when I started living my truth
along came the Gem-in-I.

I see the gem in you
Do you see the Gem-in-I?
I see the gem will shine
Let that river cry.

That's called the Gem-in-I.
I see the Gem-in-I.
I see the gem in you
We see the Gem-in-I.

The Great Manifestation

I wish upon the brightest star
dreaming of life
with my beautiful wife
and amazing kids,
wrapped in joy and purpose.

Abundance blooms in the garden
fruits and veggies
standing tall in raised beds,
dancing to the rhythm
of watery soil,
kissed by the rising sun.

A go-kart track
winds through backyard dirt trails,
ATVs and mules
racing our hearts out
pouring fun into the air
like songs from the soil.

Acres of sacred land
stretch across the quiet,
where you could hear a fly fart
and the wind
whirlpools hymns
through nature's breath.

Home-cooked meals
from garden harvests,
fresh-squeezed orange juice
in a chilled glass
on a sunlit breakfast bar.

Imagine your wildest dreams
manifesting
like autumn leaves

falling from summer's heat,
gracefully drifting
without winter's blizzard.

The inner magician awakens
creating word magic,
writing and speaking
your grandest visions
into existence.

Stars sit in the heavens
with notepads in hand,
recording your intentions
to send them back as CME's
solar kisses
that rain your wishes
onto your crown.

So magic
takes its course
through the palm of your hands,
guided by the stroke
of the mightiest sword,
as your words
lift off the page

Star-dusting their way
into physical form,
with intuition as the courier
delivering every vision
into the mighty I Am.

Affirming:
It is said.
It is so.
It is done.
And so it shall be.

Next Phase

I envision heightened awareness
within beings of righteousness,
climbing beyond the lens
of blinded eyes bound to sin.

Once you realize
December was deception
a false turning of the year,
where nature bore the weight
of winter's unseen harvest

You will know:
we survived the greatest battle,
not by sword nor shield,
but by the quiet brilliance within.

They mirrored you.
They belittled your wisdom,
their crooked smiles
hiding centuries of self hatred.

Yet you carried on
the weight of your past,
the riddles of your present,
and the ember of a brighter dawn.

You never surrendered to the noise.
Even when tears
slithered down the blanket of your face,
you wiped them away
and with a knowing smile,
you remembered:
this is not your fate.

You were always destined
for the next phase.

And beyond this volume,
the center of Self awaits

Message To My Soul Tribe

Remember—healing is a journey, not a race. Life will always have its ups and downs, but with patience you'll find your rhythm. Peel back your layers gently, with compassion for yourself. The experiences that shook your world are not just wounds; they are stories, lessons, and wisdom you can share with others. Never dim your light to make others comfortable, not even those tied to your pain. Their inability to see your worth came from their own hurt and projections, not because you lacked anything. That was never your fault. Keep choosing to be the change you want to see. Make your impact felt in the spaces you enter. You are not in the background of life, you are the main character. You deserve the spotlight. So rise, take action, and create a life that brings you unity, love, abundance, prosperity, and all things divine—daily in abundance. It is said. It is so. It is done. Thus it shall be.